Alez learns about Germs

By Karen Allen Howard

Illustrated By Debbie J Hefke

Empire Publishing
www.empirebookpublishing.com

Dedication

To my grandchildren, Tyler, Wyatt, Ryker, Rayna, and River.

Hi I'm Alez!

I have to stay home because of **invisible GERMS** that are making the whole world sick.

Mom, Mike the mailman is delivering a package, but why does he look like that?

Mom, why can't I hug Mike the mailman? Alez's Mom said that they all had to keep their distance to keep everyone **safe from the germs** that could make them sick.

Watching her Mom **spray the package** with germ spray stuff, Alez opened the box after it dried and found puzzles and books inside.

Alez's Mom asked Alez to go wash her
hands after she looked at the books!

I had to sit in the car while my Mom went in the store with a mask on.

I watched my mom put all the groceries in the
trunk of the car then she got in and took
off **her mask.**

I wanted to be a good helper, but I had to put hand **sanitizer** on my hands when we got back from the store. I sat in the kitchen while my Mom and Dad wiped all of the groceries down with this towel thingy that kills germs..

Mom and Dad were singing **Happy Birthday** and **ABC** 's with bubbles foaming on their hands in the sink.

My Mom and Dad taught me how to stay safe from the **invisible germs** and **have fun** at the same time!

I got my own **sanitizer** in a rainbow case.

Alez has her own **mask!** Her parents got her a
beautiful mask with fruit on it so she could go
to the store sometime soon.

She would have to stay **6 feet away** from
others to stay safe and keep others safe
from the germs.

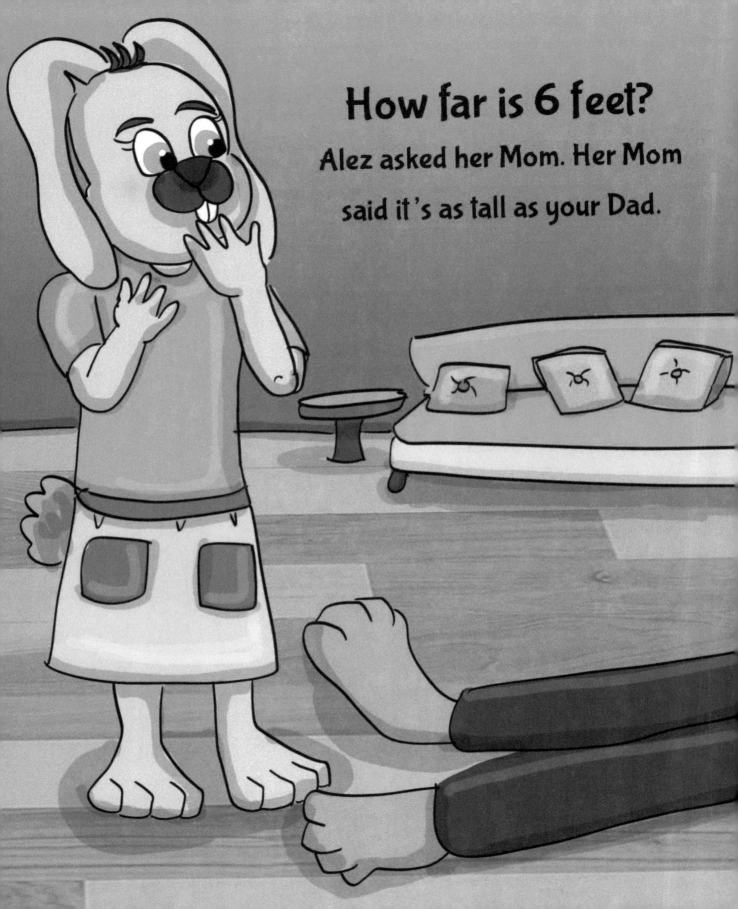

How far is 6 feet?

Alez asked her Mom. Her Mom said it's as tall as your Dad.

I went to the grocery store with
Mom **today!** We followed these arrows
on the floor. We stood on stickers on the floor waiting
our turn to move forward. The nice cashier was behind
a plastic window when we were paying.

When I got home **I washed my hands** singing. . .

ABCDEFGHIJKLMNO
PQRSTWXYZ

now I know my ABC's and now I'm clean.

I'm learning how to be safe in our new world.

How Do I Keep Germs Away from Me?

Wash my hands often AND when my parents and teachers ask me to.

Wear my mask when I go out.

Don't touch my face in public while wearing a mask.

Keep my hands to myself, don't touch anything.

Stay at least 6 feet away from others when I go out.

Use hand sanitizer when my parents and teachers ask me too.

About the Author

Karen Howard lives in Southern Illinois. She has two daughters, a son, and five grandchildren, and has been a nurse for over 35 years. Karen comes from a family of writers, including brother TJ Howard, and sister, Shirley Roney. Howard was inspired to write "Alez Learns About Germs" as she faced her young grandchildren's questions amidst the COVID-19 pandemic.
These inquiries made her aware of a need to educate curious young children about germs, and how they can affect our daily lives. The author's hope is that Alez's story will inspire parents, teachers, and adults to explore creative, fun ways to help children understand how to stay safe and healthy in our world today.

CPSIA information can be obtained
at www.ICGtesting.com
Printed in the USA
BVHW020309100920
588446BV00004B/225

9 781733 396998